ELECTRICITY AND MAGNETISM

Written by
Mike Clemmet

Illustrated by
Terry Kennett, Diane Lumley, Salvatore Tomaselli

Edited by
Caroline White

Designed by
Claire Robertson

Picture research by
Emma Segal

CONTENTS

2 The discovery of electricity

Electricity provides us with heat and light. It also works our televisions, radios, computers and high-speed trains. People have known about electricity for thousands of years, but it wasn't until the eighteenth century that scientists began to take much interest in it.

Amber is used to make jewellery.

Electricity from amber

There are lots of precious stones that are used for making jewellery. One of these stones is called amber.

You may be able to see some amber in a jeweller's shop window. It is a yellowish-brown colour. Amber is the fossilised resin from trees that lived thousands of years ago. The Ancient Greeks used it to make jewellery. They called it *elektron*.

About 2500 years ago, a Greek philosopher called Thales noticed something odd about amber. Thales found that if he rubbed a piece of amber with a cloth, it picked up small pieces of thread and fluff.

Electricity from glass

In the sixteenth century, a scientist called William Gilbert noticed that if he rubbed glass with a clean dry cloth, it too attracted small pieces of fluff, thread and paper. Because amber was the first substance to be found to do this, and because the Ancient Greeks called this precious stone *elektron*, Gilbert decided to use the word 'electricity' when talking about this effect.

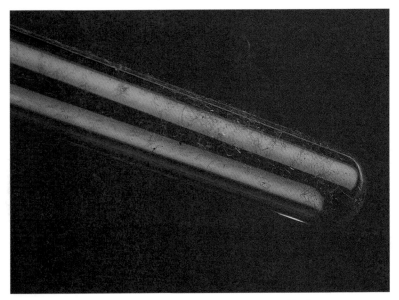

When glass is rubbed with a cloth, it attracts small pieces of thread and fluff.

Two sorts of electricity?

In 1733 a French scientist called Charles Dufay decided that there must be two sorts of electricity. He took two amber rods and rubbed them. He hung one rod up and moved the other rod towards it.

Dufay noticed that as the rods got closer together, the one that was hanging up started to move away from the other one. It was pushed away, or repelled, by it. He then did the same thing with two glass rods. They too repelled each other.

Make your own electricity

Try this for yourself. Get a comb, a clean dry cloth and some very small pieces of thread or paper. Rub the comb hard with the cloth and then hold it near the thread or paper. The pieces will 'jump' towards the comb. We say they are 'attracted' to it.

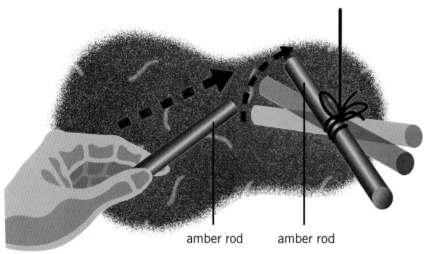

amber rod   amber rod

Amber rods that have been rubbed with a cloth will repel each other.

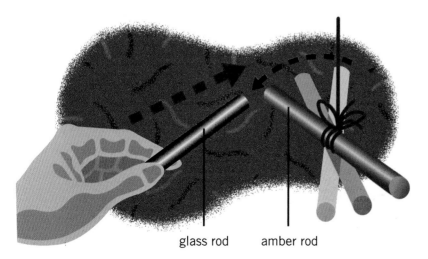

glass rod   amber rod

A glass rod and an amber rod that have been rubbed with a cloth will attract each other.

Dufay tried the same thing again, this time using one glass rod and one amber rod. The rod that was hanging up moved towards the other rod. It was attracted to it.

Dufay thought that the two amber rods must be making the same sort of electricity, and that things with the same sort of electricity must repel each other. He thought that the amber rod must be making a different sort of electricity to the glass rod, and that things with different sorts of electricity must attract one another. He called the two sorts of electricity vitreous ('from glass') and resinous ('from resin'). Today we know that there is only one sort of electricity.

Only one sort of electricity

About two hundred years ago, scientists began to make machines that could produce electricity. One of these was called the Wimshurst Machine. It was named after the man who invented it. When the handle was turned, two discs spun round and rubbed against each other. The electricity produced was collected on metal balls.

The invention of machines like this made it easier to study and use electricity. Doctors used these machines to treat their patients for all kinds of illnesses, even though they didn't really know what electricity was or how it acted.

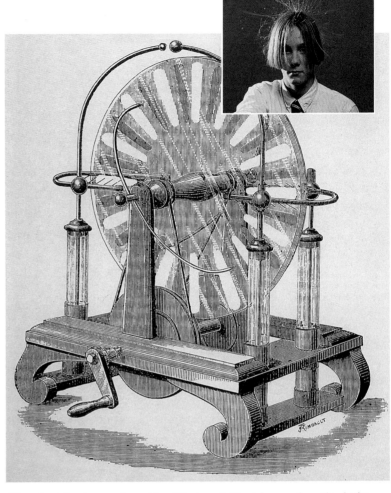

The electric charge from the Wimhurst Machine makes the hairs repel each other.

Benjamin Franklin

Scientists travelled around with these machines giving talks about electricity. They would ask someone from the audience to stand on a mat and hold the ball. As electricity went into the person's body, his or her hair would stand on end. This happened because each hair was being repelled by the other hairs.

An American statesman called Benjamin Franklin was in the audience when one of these scientists visited the United States. Franklin became so interested in electricity that he persuaded the scientist to sell him his equipment.

Positive and negative

Franklin carried out many experiments using the equipment and decided that the earlier scientists had been wrong. He decided that there was only one sort of electricity.

Franklin found that if he rubbed an amber rod, it gained electricity. This made it positively charged. If he rubbed a glass rod, electricity was taken away from it. This made it negatively charged.

When Franklin put an amber rod and a glass rod close together, he saw that electricity moved from the positively charged amber rod to the negatively charged glass rod. This equalised the charges. He could see this happening because an electric spark moved between the rods.

In the same way, Franklin saw that thunderclouds were positively charged with electricity while the surface of the Earth was negatively charged. This meant that when the clouds became full of electricity, they discharged it to Earth. The passage of electricity was seen as an electric spark, or lightning.

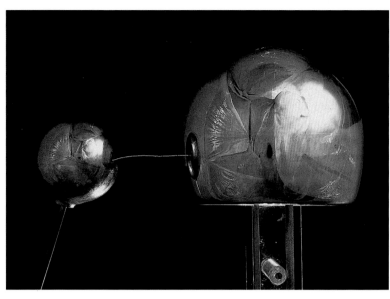

One ball has a lot of charge. The other has very little. Electricity flows between the balls to equalise the charge.

Electricity flows from cloud to ground in a lightning stroke.

Nowadays we know that the top and bottom of a cloud can have a different electrical charge. This is why there are sparks, or lightning, between clouds.

Electric charge can also flow from cloud to cloud in a lightning stroke.

Static electricity

The first materials to produce electricity were non-metals. Glass and amber are non-metals. When electricity is produced by rubbing glass or amber, it stays where it is produced. Electricity builds up on the material. It doesn't flow away or go anywhere. This is called 'static' electricity.

If you comb your hair with a plastic comb on a very dry day, your hair may seem to stick to the comb and stand up on end. The comb rubs against the hairs and produces a charge on each one. The charges are alike, so the hairs repel each other. If the room is fairly dark, you may even see faint blue sparks being produced. This does not happen if you use a metal comb.

If you rub two different materials together, an electric charge builds up on each one. One material becomes positively charged with electricity (it has more electricity than it had before). The other becomes negatively charged (it has less electricity than it had before). Eventually, if you keep rubbing, the difference in charge becomes so great that electricity flows between the two materials. They become equal in charge once more.

Static electricity is produced when the plastic comb rubs against the hairs.

Lightning

Clouds are made up of water droplets. These droplets are moving all the time. They are 'rubbing against' the air, becoming charged with electricity. If the particles are moving fast enough, they build up a very high charge. When the charge is high enough, the clouds discharge their extra electricity to the ground or to another cloud. This is seen as a huge electric spark, called lightning.

In 1752 Benjamin Franklin, the American statesman and scientist, proved that lightning is electrical. He found that all clouds, whether it was thundering or not, were charged with electricity. He did this by flying a kite in a thunderstorm.

Benjamin Franklin flew a kite during a thunderstorm. He proved that clouds are charged with electricity.

A metal key was attached to the string. When lightning struck the kite, a spark flashed as electricity passed down the wet string to the key. Franklin realised that electricity was not really 'static'. He saw that it did move – it 'flowed' along the wet string that was tied to the kite.

Using static electricity

Modern photocopiers use static electricity to make copies of pictures. The picture is scanned and the darkest parts are electrically charged on a roller. As the plain paper passes by the charged area, static electricity drags carbon powder on to the paper. The carbon is then sealed on to the paper by heat.

All tall buildings have lightning conductors.

Conductors and insulators

Franklin realised that electricity can flow through some things and not through others. He called the things that electricity can move through conductors. He called the things that electricity cannot flow though insulators. Franklin found that metals will conduct electricity and non-metals will not.

Safety from lightning

Franklin built a lightning conductor on his local church. He attached a metal spike to the highest part of the church and connected it to the ground with a thick metal rod. If lightning struck the building, it would flow through the rod to the ground, instead of causing a massive spark of lightning. Because electricity flows easily through metals, it would not produce a lot of heat, so there would be no danger of fire.

Current electricity

In 1786 an Italian scientist called Luigi Galvani used frogs to find out how muscles in the human body work. He hung the frogs on a rail round his laboratory. One day he noticed something strange. He saw that the legs sometimes twitched when he lifted them down from the rail.

People already knew from static electricity machines that electricity makes the muscles twitch. Galvani decided that the frog's legs must contain electricity. He wrote an account of what he had noticed and published it for other scientists to read.

Electricity from metals

Another Italian scientist, Alessandro Volta, became interested in animal electricity. He thought Galvani was wrong about the frogs containing a special sort of electricity. After he had read Galvani's account very carefully, he realised that the frogs were hanging on hooks made of steel and that the rail was made of brass. Maybe electricity was being made because of the two different metals and not because of the frogs?

Volta tried touching the muscle in a frog's leg with two different metals at the same time. The muscle twitched! He decided that the frog muscle wasn't needed at all.

Volta found that electricity is made by dipping two different metals in a bowl filled with a salt solution. By connecting lots of bowls together, one after the other, he could make a lot of electricity.

Luigi Galvani found out about electricity whilst working on the muscles in frog's legs.

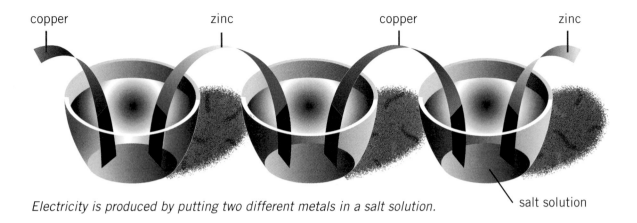

Electricity is produced by putting two different metals in a salt solution.

The trouble with this arrangement was that it took up a lot of space and could be messy. To overcome these problems, Volta made small discs of copper and zinc. He piled them up with cardboard discs that had been soaked in a salt solution. This became known as a Voltaic Pile. Electricity could be drawn off by connecting wires to the top and bottom of the Voltaic Pile.

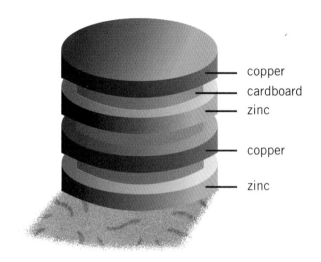

Copper and zinc discs make electricity in a Voltaic Pile.

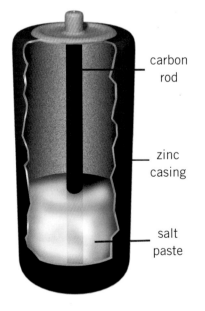

There is no liquid in a modern battery. A salt paste is used instead.

The Voltaic Pile was made up of lots of repeating units. The word 'battery' means 'lots of repeating units'. Eventually, Voltaic Piles became known as electric batteries. The unit used for measuring the strength of a battery is the volt, after Volta.

Batteries today

Modern batteries work in the same way as Volta's batteries, but they are more efficient. The most common battery has zinc and carbon in contact with a salt solution. The salt solution uses a special sort of salt – not the sort you put on your dinner. It is made into a paste so it won't spill. The zinc is the casing that holds in the paste. The carbon is a rod in the middle of the battery.

Circuits

An electric battery has two poles. One is a positive pole and the other is a negative pole. If you put a wire from the positive pole to the negative pole, electricity will flow round the wire from one end of the battery to the other. Because this was likened to the flow of water in a river, it became known as a 'current'.

If you put a wire from the positive pole of a battery to a bulb, and another wire from the bulb to the negative pole, the electric current has to flow through the bulb to get from one pole to the other. The bulb lights up. An arrangement like this, where an electric current flows from one pole to the other, is called a circuit.

Electricity flows in a loop from the positive pole of a battery to the negative pole.

Switches

If one of the wires comes loose, there will be a gap in the circuit. Electricity will stop flowing and the light will go out. Switches are used to open and close gaps in circuits. When a switch is used to break a circuit, it will stop the flow of current. When it is used to make a circuit, it will allow the current to flow through it.

This is a bit like Tower Bridge in London. When the roadway is lifted up, there is a gap in the road and the traffic stops flowing. When the roadway is lowered, the gap in the road is closed and the traffic can start flowing again.

The switch is open. Electricity cannot flow because there is a gap in the circuit.

The bridge is open. The traffic cannot flow because there is a gap in the road.

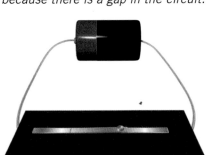

The switch is closed. Electricity can flow because there is no gap in the circuit.

The bridge is down. The traffic can flow because there is no gap in the road.

The light at the top of the stairs

Light switches at home are always on in one position and off in the other. The switches at the top and bottom of the stairs are different though. They are a special sort of switch. If the light at the top of the stairs is off, whichever switch you press, and whatever position it is in to start with, the light will go on.

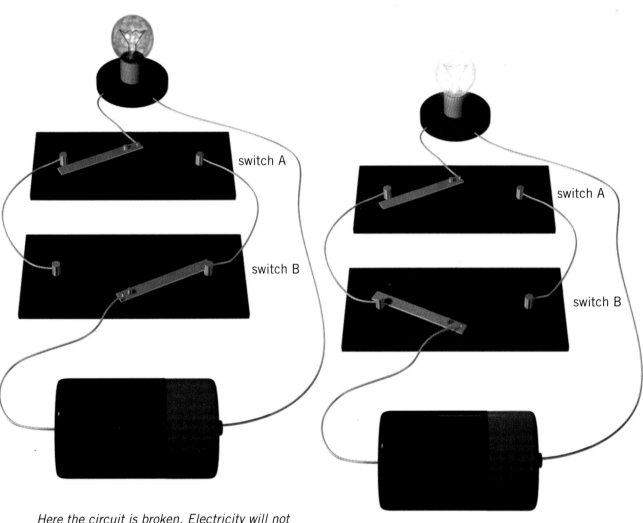

Here the circuit is broken. Electricity will not flow. Whichever switch is moved will close the circuit and the light will come on.

Here the circuit is made. Electricity will flow. Whichever switch is moved will open the circuit and the bulb will go out.

Resistance

When you close the switch on an electric circuit, a current starts to flow. The battery is the source of energy in a circuit. It pushes the current round the circuit. It is more difficult for the battery to push the current round some circuits than others.

All circuits resist the flow of electricity to some extent. We say that all circuits have resistance to the flow of the current. Suppose you have a simple circuit made up of one battery, two wires and a bulb. The bulb and wires have a certain amount of resistance.

If you put another bulb in the circuit, there will be more resistance and so less current will flow. Because there is less current, the bulbs will be dimmer. So one thing that affects the current is the number of things that it has to pass through, such as bulbs, hair dryers or electric toasters. We call these things appliances. The more appliances there are in a circuit, the greater the resistance.

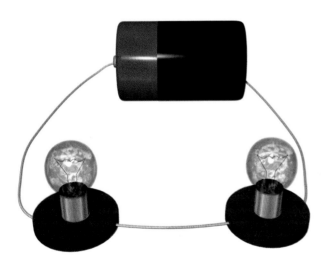

This simple circuit has two bulbs, a battery and wires.

Each piece of wire also has resistance. If you put a second piece of wire into the circuit, the resistance increases and the current is reduced. It is the same as making each piece of wire longer. The longer the circuit, the greater the resistance.

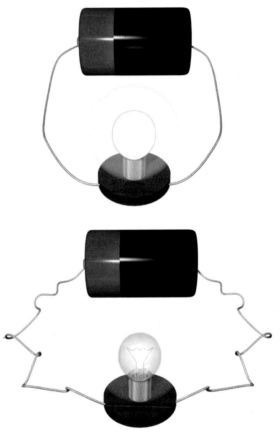

There is more resistance when the wires are longer. This makes the bulb dimmer.

The thinner the wire, the harder it is for the battery to push the current through it. The thinner the wire, the greater the resistance.

Different materials also have different resistance. Copper, for example, has less resistance than iron. This is why copper is usually used for making electric wires.

Resistors

Cars and other machines have lots of electrical components. Some of the components would get damaged if too much current passed through them. This is why a resistor is sometimes put into a circuit to cut down the current. Resistors are long lengths of wire made of materials that have high resistance. To make them easier to handle, the wire is wound into a coil.

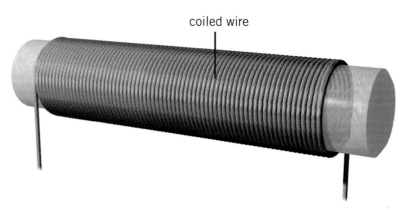

coiled wire

Resistors are made of long pieces of wire. The wire is coiled up to make the resistor easier to use.

The people who make resistors can work out exactly how much resistance they have by looking at the type of material used and the length and thickness of the wire.

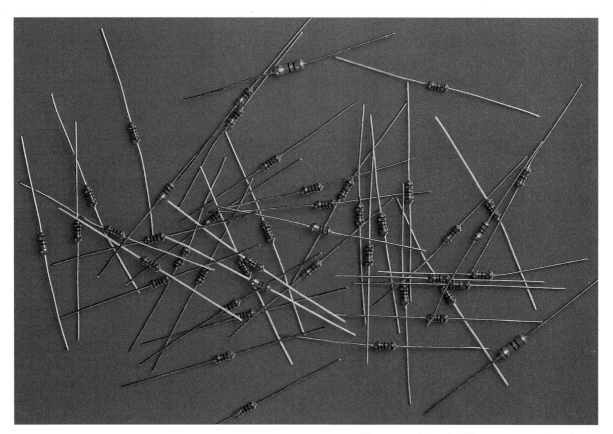

There are lots of different types of resistor.

Electrical heating

When electricity passes through a material, it produces heat. Household appliances such as kettles and toasters have heating wires in them that get very hot when electricity flows through them.

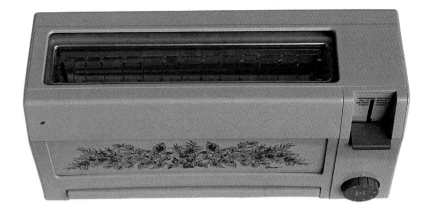

The wires inside an electric toaster get very hot and give out heat.

Heat is produced when an electric current flows through a circuit. The harder it is for the battery to push the current round the circuit, the more heat is produced. The coils in an electric fire are made of a material that has high resistance. It is hard for the electricity to flow through the wire so a lot of heat is produced. The wire glows red hot and gives out heat to warm up the room.

The element in a kettle gets hot and heats up the water.

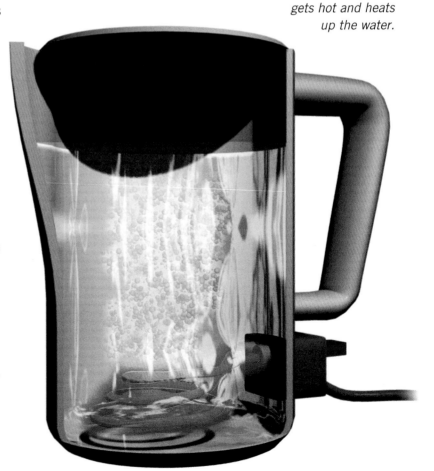

Hot water

Electric kettles have an element inside them. The element contains a wire that has high resistance. When you switch on the kettle, electricity flows through the element. This makes it hot. The heat then passes to the water in the kettle. Eventually, the water gets hot enough to boil.

Thermostats

Bath water is often heated in the same way. Many homes have an immersion heater in the hot-water tank. It is made of a coil of wire that has high resistance. As electricity flows through the heater, the coil gets hot and heats up the water around it. To stop the water getting hotter and hotter until it boils, a thermostat is used to control the temperature.

Thermostats have a strip made from two different metals. It is called a bimetallic strip. The two metals expand at different rates when heated, making the strip bend. This opens or closes the electrical circuit, switching the current on or off.

As the strip gets hot, it bends upwards. This breaks the circuit and the current stops flowing. As the water cools, the strip starts to straighten out again. This makes the circuit and the current begins to flow.

Thermostats are used in central heating systems and in cars to keep the temperature steady. They are also used in toasters, where they are part of the 'browning' control.

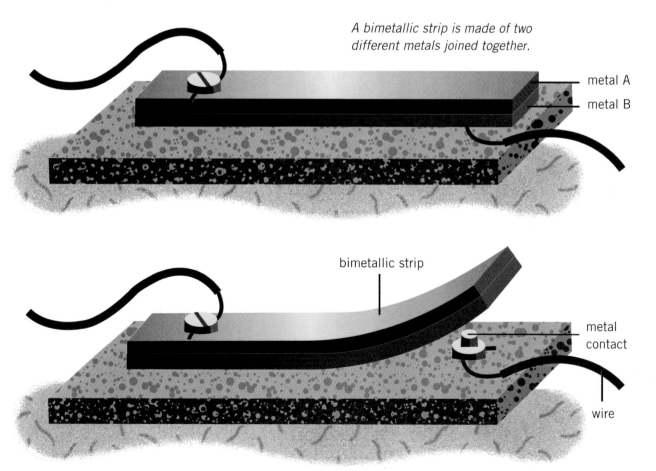

A bimetallic strip is made of two different metals joined together.

metal A

metal B

bimetallic strip

metal contact

wire

When the bimetallic strip gets hot, it bends away from the contact and cuts off the current to the heater.

Electrical lighting

When an electric current flows through a material, it produces heat. How much the material heats up depends on what it is made of, how long and thin it is and how much current is flowing. When things get hot enough, they start to give out light.

About a hundred years ago, it seemed quite easy to produce light from electricity. All you had to do was pass an electric current through a material that had high resistance. It would get hot, start to glow and give out light.

Thomas Edison

The problem was that things start to burn or melt when they get too hot. A material would have to be found that would not burn or melt when it got extremely hot – at least not for a long time, anyway.

An American inventor called Thomas Edison came up with the answer. He made a very fine line of carbon. It had such high resistance that the carbon became white hot extremely quickly when electricity was passed through it.

This metal is so hot that it gives out light.

However, the carbon also burned quickly. Edison thought, 'What do things need to burn? They need air!' He decided that if he could keep the carbon wire away from air, it would get hot but not burn.

In 1879 Edison put the thin carbon wire inside a glass bulb and took out all the air. When he connected the bulb to the electricity supply, the wire got hot, gave out light and continued to do so for forty hours before it burned out. Edison had invented a light bulb that worked for almost two days!

'Gosh, we haven't had to change this bulb for a whole day!'

Modern light bulbs last for months. The filament is made of tungsten, which doesn't burn out easily.

Longer life

Light bulbs work in exactly the same way today. Inside each bulb is a very thin wire called a filament. When you switch on a light, electricity flows through the filament. It gets so hot that it starts to give out light.

Filaments are no longer made of carbon. Carbon filaments are fragile and break if they are shaken even slightly. Nowadays the filament is made of tungsten, which is a lot tougher than carbon.

The contents of the bulb are also different. Edison took out all the air from the bulb to stop the filament burning. Today light bulbs are filled with a gas called argon. Argon does not react with anything. The filament can get very hot and it still won't react with the argon around it. Modern light bulbs will work for months and not burn out.

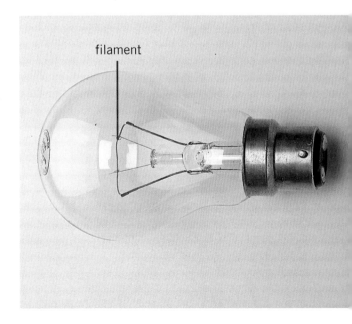

filament

The metal in a filament is very fine. It is coiled up so that a long length of wire will fit into a small space.

Danger!

The human body conducts electricity, but it has high resistance. An ordinary battery is not powerful enough to drive an electric current through your body.

Struck by lightning

In a thunderstorm, the clouds get charged with electricity. The difference between the charge on the clouds and the charge on the ground becomes so high that electricity flows through the air from cloud to ground or from ground to cloud. As electricity passes through the air, the air heats up by thousands of degrees. We see this as a stroke of lightning.

Anything that sticks up above the ground will attract lightning.

If you are standing outside during a thunderstorm, your body will become charged with electricity. Because the difference in charge between your body and the clouds is so high, electricity may flow through you. In other words, you may be hit by a stroke of lightning. As the enormous current flows through your body, it heats you up and can burn or kill you.

Anything that sticks out of the ground, such as a tree, church tower or chimney, is more likely to be struck by lightning than the flat ground.

Stay safe

You should never shelter under a tree during a thunderstorm, even if it means getting wet! The safest thing to do is to lie down or crouch down until the storm has passed.

Power lines

The power lines that you see running between pylons carry a very high electrical current. The current is high enough to pass through your body and kill you. This is why you should never climb pylons or fly kites or use fishing rods near power lines. If you touch a power line with a kite string or a rod, the current will flow through it and then through you. The power lines that carry the current to drive trains are also dangerous.

The mains electricity cable in your home does not carry as much current as the power lines, but it can still kill you. You should never touch a bare wire in your home.

Power lines carry high electric currents. If you touch one, the current can flow through your body and kill you.

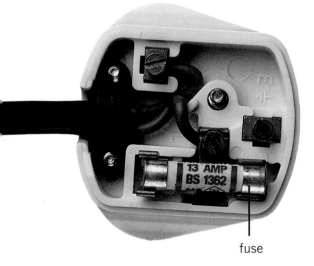

fuse

The fuse in this plug will burn out if there is too much current. It will stop all current flowing.

Fuses

Sometimes things go wrong with electrical equipment and too much current starts to flow. This produces a lot of heat and can start a fire.

Look at the fuse in the plug opposite. A fuse is made of very thin wire and is designed to melt if too much current flows through it. This breaks the circuit and stops electricity flowing. It is better for the fuse to melt than for a fire to start.

Circuit diagrams

Electrical engineers design circuits for machines such as cars, washing machines and fridges. They have to be able to tell other people how to make the circuits.

The engineers could write out instructions. But that would take a long time, and people who speak a different language might not understand them. They could do it by drawing pictures. But these would look complicated, and different countries might have different sorts of appliances or batteries.

This is why circuit diagrams are used to show other people how to set up circuits. Circuit diagrams contain symbols for the different appliances. The symbols are international. Scientists and electricians around the world know what they mean. Some of the symbols can be seen below.

There are lots of different sorts of battery.

This symbol means a battery or cell. The long stroke represents the positive pole. The short stroke represents the negative pole. All batteries are represented by the same symbol.

This symbol means a switch. All switches are represented by the same symbol.

There are lots of different sorts of switch.

This symbol means a lamp or bulb. All bulbs are represented by the same symbol.

There are lots of different sorts of bulb.

A drawing of a circuit that has a battery, a switch and a bulb might look like this:

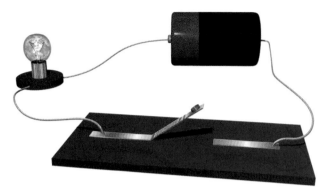

Here is another circuit diagram. It has two lamps that come one after the other in the circuit. Appliances that are connected one after the other are said to be connected in series.

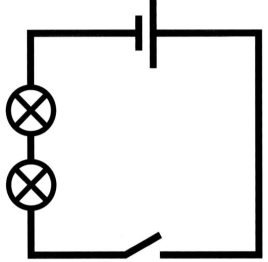

The circuit diagram would look like this:

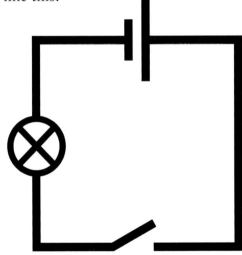

If you had the materials, you could use this diagram to make the circuit below.

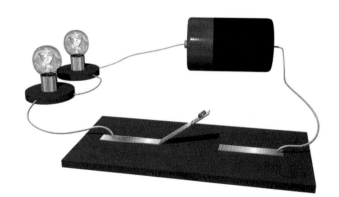

This diagram tells you that there is a wire going from the positive pole of the battery to a switch. There is also a wire going from the other side of the switch to a bulb, and another wire going from the other side of the bulb back to the battery.

Wires are always drawn as straight lines, even though they probably aren't straight in the real circuit. Straight lines look neater and make it easier to understand the diagram.

Series and parallel circuits

There are two sorts of Christmas tree light sets. With one sort, it doesn't matter if one of the bulbs goes out because the others will stay on. This is a parallel circuit. With the other sort, if one bulb goes out, they all go out. This is a series circuit.

Series circuits

In a series circuit, it is difficult to find which bulb has failed. All you can do is replace the bulbs one by one until you get to the right one. Why does this happen?

The bulbs are connected one after the other in the circuit along a single wire. When things are connected like this, we say they are in series.

Christmas tree lights can be connected in series or in parallel.

If a bulb fails, the current cannot flow through it. This means there is a break in the circuit and the current stops flowing altogether. All the other bulbs go out even though there is nothing wrong with them.

These bulbs are connected in series with one another.

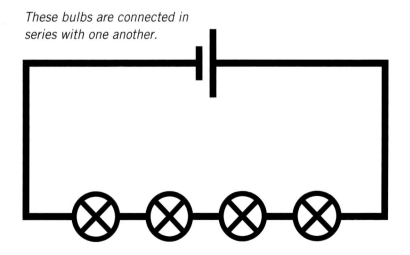

There are several things that can make a bulb fail. The filament can break or burn out, or one of the connections to the bulb can become loose. Whatever the reason, the current will stop flowing through that bulb.

Many torches use two batteries connected in series. You have to be careful to connect the batteries the right way round. The positive end of one battery must be connected to the negative end of the other battery. If you connect two positive ends together, the batteries will try to push the current in opposite directions and no current will flow. When two batteries are joined the right way round, each one pushes the current in the same direction.

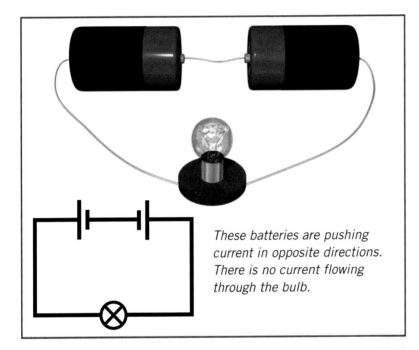

These batteries are pushing current in opposite directions. There is no current flowing through the bulb.

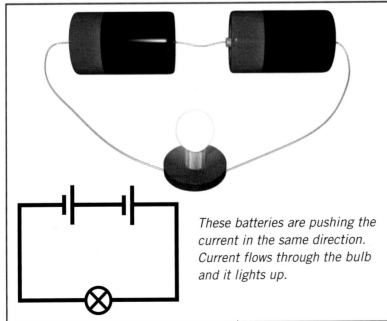

These batteries are pushing the current in the same direction. Current flows through the bulb and it lights up.

Parallel circuits

Imagine what would happen if the lights in your home were connected in series. If one bulb failed, all the other lights would go out as well. Electricians avoid this by connecting the lights in parallel with each other. If one bulb fails, the others keep working. This is done by splitting the circuit into branches.

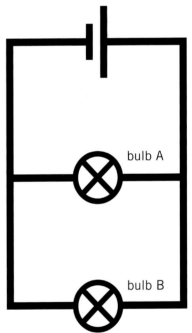

These bulbs are connected in parallel. If bulb A fails, the current will still flow through bulb B. This means that only bulb A will go out.

Dimming the lights

In theatres, the stage lights often need to be made gradually brighter or dimmer during a play. To make the lights brighter, all you have to do is pass more current through the bulbs. To dim the lights, you pass less current through the bulbs. How can you do this?

Dimmer switches are found behind the scenes in theatres.

Changing resistance

The longer a wire is, the greater its resistance to the flow of electricity. This means there will be less current going through the wire. So one way to dim a bulb is to keep connecting it to longer and longer lengths of wire.

However, you cannot keep changing the length of wire during the performance of a play, particularly while the electricity is switched on. This is why a long coil of

wire is used with a contact that you can slide along it. The further the contact is from the electricity supply, the greater the length of wire that the current has to flow through. This makes the resistance higher and the bulb dimmer.

To make the lights brighter, all you have to do is slide the contact closer to the electricity supply.

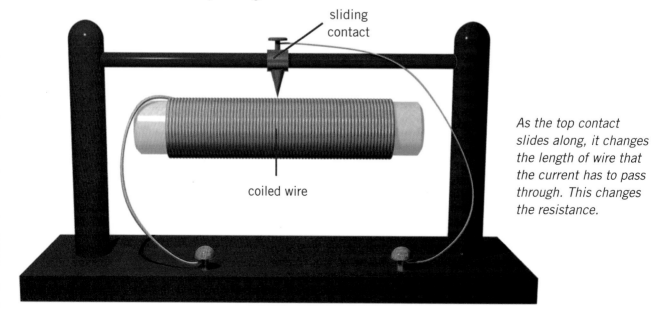

sliding contact

coiled wire

As the top contact slides along, it changes the length of wire that the current has to pass through. This changes the resistance.

Some materials conduct electricity better than others. Copper is a good conductor. A very long piece of copper wire would have to be used to get the resistance high enough to dim the bulb. This is why the wire is made out of a material that has high resistance.

A straight piece of wire would take up a lot of space, and you would have to slide the contact a long way to dim the bulb. This is why the wire is curled up.

These coiled wires are called variable resistors because their resistance can be changed. Variable resistors aren't just used in theatres. Lots of people have them at home to make the lights brighter or dimmer.

Some electric drills also use variable resistors. This allows them to go faster or slower gradually.

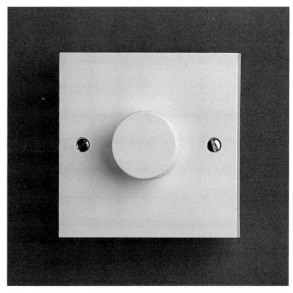

Does your home have a dimmer switch?

Electric drills have a variable resistor to make them go faster or slower.

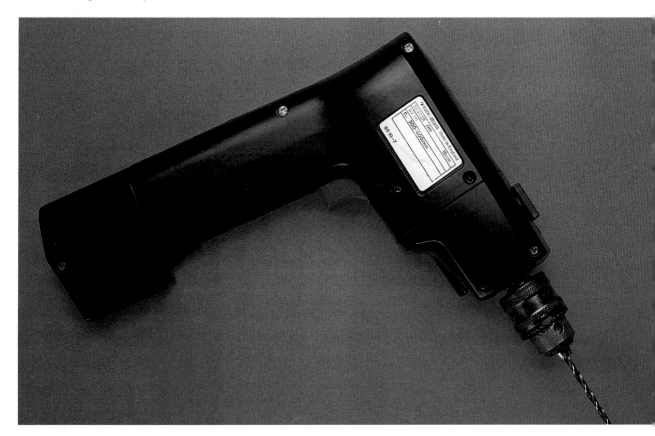

Magnets

Over two thousand years ago in Ancient Greece, some stones were found that behaved oddly. They were attracted to iron and to each other. The stones were known as lodestones. Today we call them magnets. Magnets get their name from the Ancient Greek town of Magnesia where many of the stones were found.

If a magnetised needle is allowed to move freely, one end will always end up pointing North.

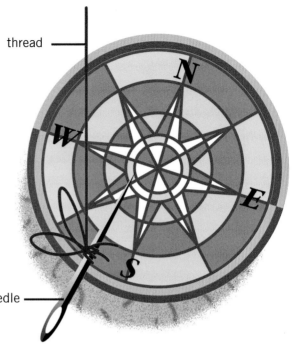

thread

magnetised needle

Making magnets

The Ancient Greeks soon discovered that the magnetism of a lodestone could be passed on to other things. They found that if they stroked an iron or steel needle in one direction with a lodestone, it became magnetic.

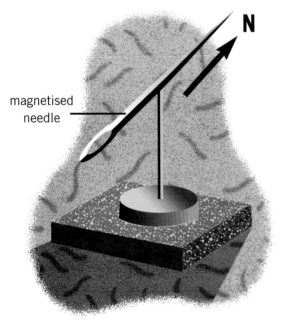

N

magnetised needle

A magnetised needle balanced on a pivot will always end up with one end pointing North.

They later found that if the needle was hung up and allowed to move freely, it would always stop with one end pointing roughly North. Another way of doing this was to balance the needle on a pivot and to let it swivel freely. Again, the needle would always come to rest pointing roughly North-South.

Eventually, someone realised that the balanced magnetic needle could be put in a box and carried on a ship. The box helped sailors to find their way at sea. No one knows who came up with this idea first of all. It might have been the Chinese or the Arabs. All we know is that it was used in Europe about eight hundred years ago. We still use magnetic needles like this in compasses today.

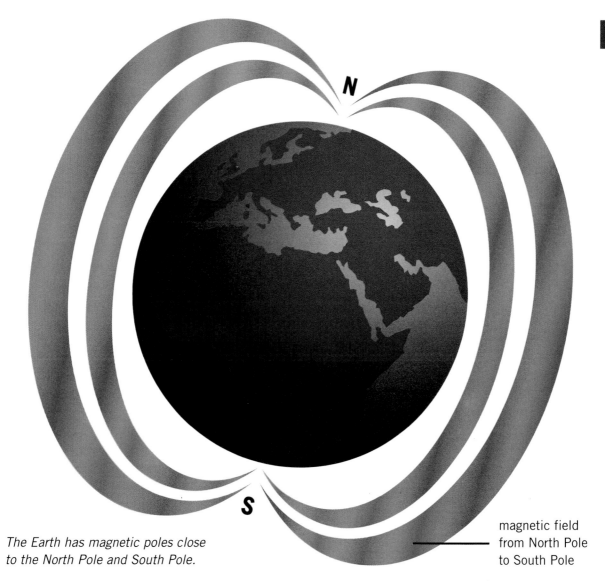

The Earth has magnetic poles close to the North Pole and South Pole.

———— magnetic field from North Pole to South Pole

Magnetic poles

One end of a magnetic needle always points North. This end should really be called the North-seeking pole, but usually we just call it the North pole. If one end of the magnet points North, the other must point South. This end is called the South pole of the magnet.

People have always wondered why one end of a magnet is attracted to the North. Because magnets were known to attract each other, some people said there must be a giant mountain made of lodestone at the North Pole of the Earth. We now know that the whole Earth acts like a giant magnet. The Earth has magnetic poles close to the North Pole and the South Pole.

In this modern compass, the needle always points North-South.

Force fields

If you put a handful of steel pins on a table and slowly bring a magnet towards them, the pins begin to move towards the magnet. It takes a force to make any object start moving. There must be forces in the space around the magnet.

You cannot see the magnetic force of a magnet. It is an invisible force that attracts some things and repels others. We call this region around the magnet a force field.

This tin can must be made of steel because it is attracted by a magnet.

Magnetic materials

Charities will sometimes collect empty aluminium drinks cans to recycle. You can tell whether a can is made of aluminium or steel by holding a magnet to it. Steel is attracted to the magnet. Aluminium is not.

Magnets do not attract all substances. They will only pick up things that contain iron, cobalt or nickel. Magnets attract steel because it is mostly made of iron.

Attraction and repulsion

If you put two North poles or two South poles on a smooth surface, you will feel the magnets pushing each other apart. We say the magnets repel each other. On the other hand, a North pole and a South pole attract each other.

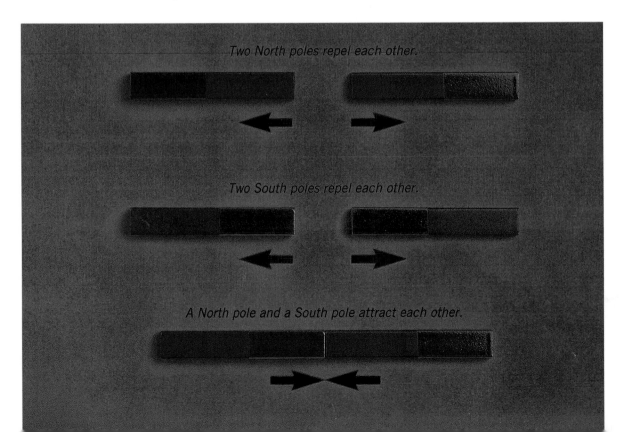

Two North poles repel each other.

Two South poles repel each other.

A North pole and a South pole attract each other.

Lines of force

If a piece of paper is placed over a magnet and iron powder sprinkled on top, each piece of iron will be attracted to the magnet. If the paper is tapped gently, the iron will form a pattern.

The pattern is made up of lines running from the North pole of the magnet to the South pole. We call these lines of force. All magnets have lines of force, but you cannot usually see them.

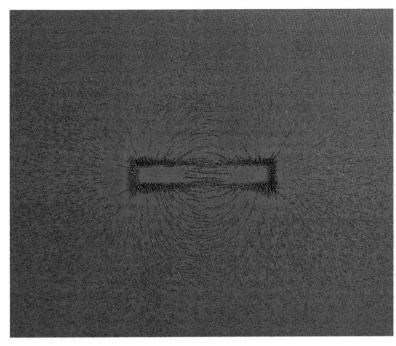

Small particles of iron settle along the magnet's lines of force.

The Earth acts like a giant magnet. It has lines of force running from the North Magnetic Pole to the South Magnetic Pole. These lines of force are what make a compass needle turn until it points North-South.

The sun also acts like a giant magnet. When hot matter is thrown out by the sun, the matter follows the lines of force round the sun. Special telescopes can take pictures of this.

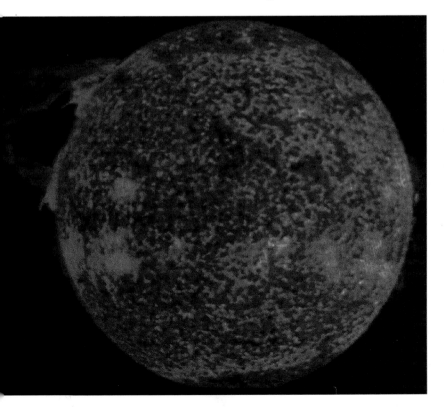

Hot matter follows the sun's lines of magnetic force.

In 1819 a Danish scientist called Hans Christian Oersted noticed something odd. He was working with electrical equipment and there was a compass sitting on the bench next to him. He saw that when he switched on the current, the needle of the compass jerked. It seemed there was a connection between electricity and magnetism.

In 1820 a French scientist called André Ampère proved that two parallel wires carrying current in the same direction will attract each other. He found they repelled each other when the current flowed in different directions. The wires were behaving just like magnets!

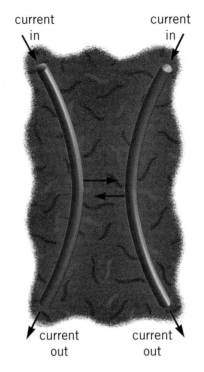

current in · current in

current out · current out

When current flows in the same direction through two parallel wires, the wires attract each other.

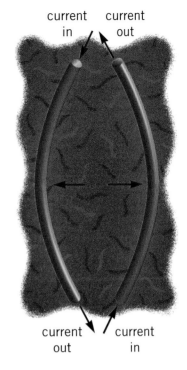

current in · current out

current out · current in

When current flows in opposite directions through two parallel wires, they repel each other.

current in

needle

wire

current out

These compass needles point clockwise round the wire. This is because the lines of force round the wire are circular.

If you move a compass round a wire carrying an electric current, the compass needle will always swing round as if next to a strong magnet. This is because the electric current is creating its own magnetic field round the wire.

If you look along the wire in the same direction as the current is flowing, the North pole of the compass needle will always point clockwise round the wire. We say that the lines of force run clockwise round the wire.

Electromagnets

Ampère realised that if the wire was wound into a coil, the lines of force would be like those of an ordinary magnet, but you would be able to switch this magnet on and off. These strong magnets that can be turned on and off as easily as an electric current are called electromagnets.

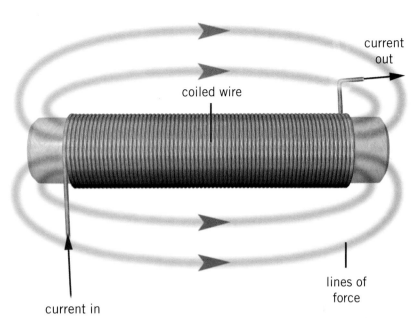

current out

coiled wire

lines of force

current in

The lines of force round each part of the coiled wire build up to make the same pattern as you would find round an ordinary magnet.

Electromagnets are used to pick up iron and steel in scrapyards.

Using electromagnets

Electromagnets have lots of uses. In recycling metals they can be used to separate iron and steel from other metals. When the electromagnet is switched on, iron and steel are attracted to it but other metals are not.

Cars contain electromagnets. When you switch on the engine, an electromagnet pulls a gear from the starter motor into position to turn over the engine.

In hospitals, doctors can use powerful electromagnets to remove small pieces of iron or steel from a patient's eye.

The electric telegraph

Two hundred years ago, most people in the United States lived near either the East or West coast. In between lay thousands of miles of prairies, deserts and mountains. This made it very difficult to get messages from one side of the country to the other. Letters were sent by coach or pony express. This took days, if not weeks.

Two hundred years ago, the only way to get a message across the United States was by horse.

Sending messages

Electricity travels very quickly along a wire. If a wire could be connected from one side of the United States to the other, the current would cover the distance in seconds. But how could it be used to send messages?

Suppose you have a switch at one end of the wire. Pressing the switch will turn the current on. Letting go of the switch will turn it off. And suppose there is a coil of wire at the other end of the wire. When the current is turned on, the coil becomes a magnet. Below the coil is a small steel bar. The bar is attracted to the coil as long as the current is flowing. As the bar moves up, it hits a stop and makes a noise. Now you have a way of sending messages. You can make the bar at the other end of the wire 'click' as it moves up and down.

Telegraph wires stretch across the countryside to carry messages by electricity.

Morse Code

The time between the clicks can be long or short. A short space of time is called a dot. A long space of time is called a dash. Each letter in the alphabet has a number of dots or dashes. The letter 's' is three dots. The letter 'o' is three dashes. The man who invented this code was called Samuel Morse. It became known as Morse Code.

Electricity and electromagnets made it possible to send messages across hundreds of miles. This is called telegraphy. The word has two parts. 'Tele' means 'distance' and 'graphy' means 'writing'. The whole word means 'writing at a distance'. Telegraph poles and wires were soon put up across many countries.

Messages under the sea

In 1850 the first cable was laid under the English Channel so that telegraph messages could be sent between Britain and Europe.

By 1858, 2300 miles of cable connected Britain to the United States, and it was possible to send messages under the Atlantic Ocean.

Just over a hundred years ago, cables were laid under the sea to carry messages between countries.

Making electricity

Electricity was first made using batteries based on Volta's copper and zinc piles. These batteries were expensive because the chemicals used were not common or cheap. Eventually, a way was found to make electricity without batteries.

In the 1830s, an English scientist called Michael Faraday became interested in the connection between electricity and magnetism. He knew that when a current flowed through a wire, a magnetic field formed round the wire. He knew that when the wire was coiled, it acted like a normal magnet. Faraday thought that if an electric current could make a magnetic field, then a magnetic field ought to be able to make an electric current.

Electricity from coils

Faraday made two coils of wire and put them close together. He connected the first coil to a battery. When he switched on the current in the first coil, a current was formed in the second coil, but it soon died away. He realised that when the current was switched on, the magnetic field round the first coil grew. The lines of force spread outwards from the wire. They 'cut through' the second coil and this made a current flow in the second coil.

When the current in the first coil stopped growing, the lines of force stopped moving outwards. They stopped 'cutting through' the second coil. The current in the second coil stopped flowing.

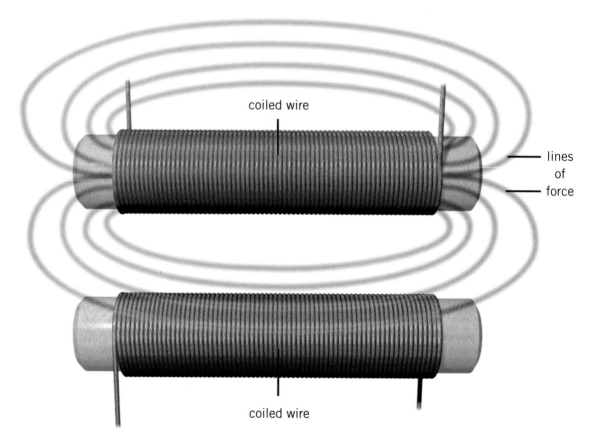

coiled wire

lines of force

coiled wire

When the current in the first coil is turned on, a magnetic field starts to form. The lines of force spread out and 'cut through' the second coil.

Electricity from moving magnets

Faraday then made a coil of wire and pushed a magnet in and out of it. As the magnet moved, the lines of force 'cut through' the coil.

Current flowed through the coil. It flowed one way as the magnet was pushed in, and the other way as the magnet was pulled out.

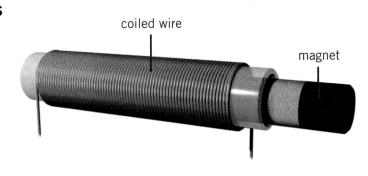

coiled wire

magnet

As the magnet moves into the coil, current flows one way. As the magnet moves out, current flows the other way.

Generators

Nowadays generators use this effect to produce electricity. Energy from fuel or from wind or water is used to turn the coils. The coils move through magnetic fields. The lines of force 'cut through' the coils and electric current is produced.

As with Faraday's experiment, the current in the coils flows one way and then the other. This is known as alternating current. The electricity that comes into our homes through the mains is alternating current. This is because less energy is lost when electricity is transmitted over long distances in this way.

When you use a battery, the current flows only one way – from the positive pole to the negative pole of the battery. This is known as direct current.

Generators provide most of our electricity. This generator is in a power station.

Electric motors

Look around your home and you will find lots of things that have electric motors in them. Tape recorders, vacuum cleaners, washing machines and hair dryers all work by electric motor.

A motor makes things move inside a machine. The movement is brought about by a current. The current is electromagnetic. It is produced by coils of wire spinning in an electric field.

All these machines use electric motors.

Movement from electricity

If you hang a thin wire between the two poles of a magnet and pass a current through it, the wire jerks to one side. If you pass a current through the wire the other way, it jerks to the other side. If you pass an alternating current through the wire, it moves from side to side, because an alternating current flows first one way and then the other.

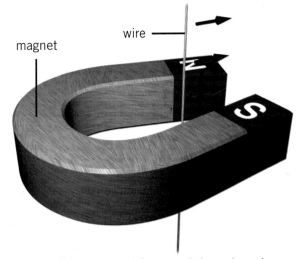

When current is passed through a wire in a magnetic field, the wire moves.

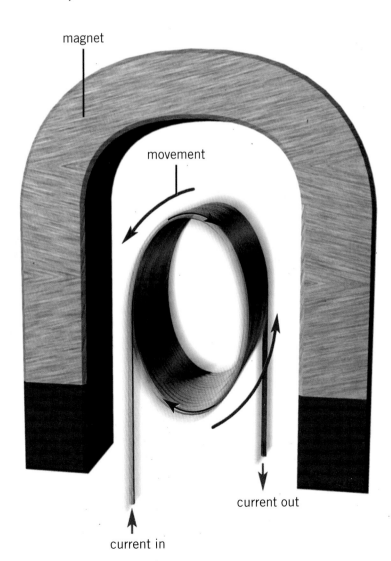

This movement of a single wire is not strong enough to drive a motor. But if you coil up the wire, the current passes through the magnetic field many times. The current in the top of the coil flows in one direction, and the current in the bottom of the coil flows in the other direction. The top of the coil moves one way, and the bottom moves the other way. It makes the coil start to spin. This movement can be used to drive an axle to turn wheels. It is an electric motor.

An electric motor works because the top and bottom of the coil move in opposite directions.

Sending sound messages

Each sound that you hear is created by vibrations. When you speak, the vocal cords at the back of your throat vibrate. This makes the air vibrate. These vibrations are transmitted through the air to your ears, where they make the eardrum vibrate.

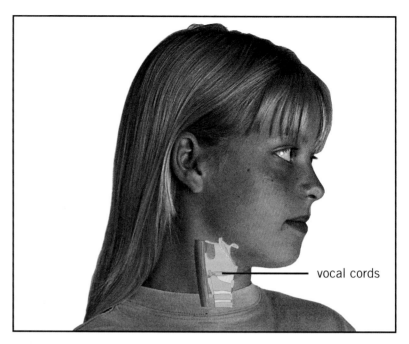

vocal cords

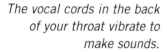
The vocal cords in the back of your throat vibrate to make sounds.

The telephone was invented just over a hundred years ago.

The first telephone

In 1876 Alexander Graham Bell found a way of carrying these vibrations in an electric signal. He invented the telephone.

Bell put a thin sheet of metal called a diaphragm in the mouthpiece. When someone spoke into the phone, the metal vibrated. These vibrations were changed into an electric current that went along a wire to the other phone. As the current passed through the second phone, its diaphragm vibrated in exactly the same pattern. The vibration of the metal produced sound – the same sound that was going into the first phone.

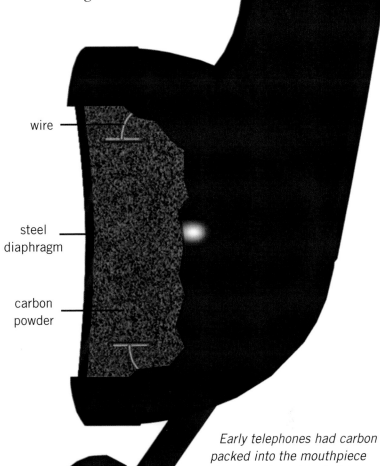

wire

steel diaphragm

carbon powder

Early telephones had carbon packed into the mouthpiece to help conduct electricity.

Improving the telephone

The first telephones did not work very well. Scientists worked hard to improve them. The first thing they did was to change the mouthpiece. They packed the space behind the diaphragm with carbon powder. Carbon conducts electricity. As the diaphragm vibrated, it moved against the carbon. This helped the carbon to conduct electricity. Nowadays, telephones and microphones use special crystals to change sound vibrations into electric currents.

Recording sound

To make records, the electric currents from the microphone pass through an electromagnet. This makes a cutter vibrate as it cuts grooves in the record.

Loudspeakers

In a loudspeaker, the diaphragm vibrates as the electric current passes through it, just like the earpiece of a telephone.

Producing electricity

Electricity is a vital part of our lives. While we sleep, it keeps the food cool in our fridges and freezers; it keeps the clock going on the central heating; it works the alarm that tells us when it's time to get up. The demand for electricity shoots up first thing in the morning as the central heating comes on and people switch on electric fires, radios and televisions and begin to make breakfast.

When people get up in the morning, they begin to use more electricity.

Where does electricity come from?

Electricity is produced in power stations. It is made by huge coils of wire spinning inside a magnetic field. This happens inside lots of generators.

Heat into movement

Where does the energy come from to turn the huge coils of wire? Most generators are turned by steam. Water is boiled and the steam blows through the blades of a turbine, which is like a giant fan. The blades spin round and turn the coils.

Burning fuels

Where does the heat come from to boil the water? In most power stations, it is produced by burning fuels. Coal, oil and natural gas are fuels.

The problem with producing electricity by burning fuels is that it puts fumes and gases into the air. Some of these cause acid rain and affect the climate. Another problem is that fossil fuels are non-renewable. You cannot make new coal and oil overnight. It takes millions of years for them to form.

Renewable sources of energy

People are now looking for other ways to turn the generators. They are looking for ways that use renewable sources of energy.

In places with lots of fast-flowing streams and rivers, water can be used to turn the turbines. This is called hydroelectric generation. But not everywhere has enough water to do this.

Wind power is sometimes used. But not everywhere has enough wind, and the wind doesn't blow all the time. Some people also think that fields of giant windmills spoil the countryside.

In other places, the sun's heat is used to boil the water and produce steam. But not everywhere gets enough sunshine.

In some countries, such as New Zealand and Iceland, hot water and steam from below the Earth's surface are used to turn the generators. But there aren't many places in the world where there is enough heat below the ground to make steam.

Wind power can be used to make electricity.

Using less energy

If we want to cut down on the use of fuels, the easiest thing to do is to use less electricity. We can stop wasting heat and light.

Falling water turns turbines to generate electricity.

Electroplating

Things aren't always what they seem. Objects that look as if they are made of silver may only be coated with it. Electricity is used to do the coating.

Most people have steel cutlery for everyday use at home. Some people may also have knives and forks for special occasions that looks like silver but aren't really. They are silver plated and are made of steel coated with a thin layer of silver.

Protecting steel

Steel is sometimes coated with other metals just to make it look more attractive. Sometimes it is done to stop the steel rusting. Tins are called 'tins' because they are made of steel coated with tin. To make the tin plate, sheets of steel are dipped into molten tin. When the sheets are pulled out, the tin sticks to the surface. The hot tin plate can then be rolled out, cut up and made into tins.

This decorative knife and fork are made of steel coated with silver.

These cans are made of steel coated with tin.

Looking good

Tins are simple shapes. It doesn't matter how even the coating of tin is as long as it is thick enough to stop the steel going rusty. Knives and forks are different. They are complicated shapes and the coating of silver needs to be even.

The best way to get an even coating of silver is to use electricity. If you look at silver cutlery, you may be able to find the letters EPNS on the blade of a knife. EP stands for 'electroplated'.

The letters EPNS tell you that electricity has been used to coat this spoon with silver.

Coating steel cutlery

The steel cutlery is placed in a tank with a liquid that conducts electricity. The cutlery is then connected to the negative pole of an electricity supply. Pure silver is put into the tank and connected to the positive pole. Silver particles are pulled off the silver and attracted across to the cutlery, where they form an even coating.

Copper plating

Take a battery, some wires, an old knife, salt and a 2p piece. Dissolve as much salt as you can in the water. Use the wire to connect the 2p piece to the positive pole of the battery and the knife blade to the negative pole. Put the 2p piece and the knife blade in the salty water and leave them for a while. You should find that the blade of the knife becomes coated with copper.

This cutlery is being silver plated. The silver dissolves and is deposited on the cutlery.

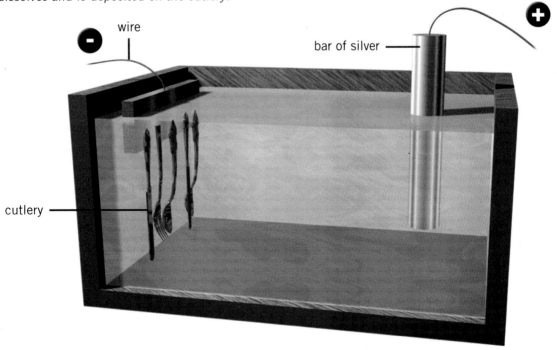

Extracting aluminium

Just over a hundred years ago, Napoleon the Third, the Emperor of France, dined off aluminium plates. Aluminium was very expensive in those days. Nowadays we think of it as a cheap metal. We use aluminium to make lots of everyday things, such as saucepans and cooking foil.

Aluminium is used to make cooking foil and saucepans.

Why was aluminium so dear?

If there isn't very much of something, it usually makes it expensive. For example, diamonds cost a lot of money because there isn't much diamond in the Earth's crust. Aluminium, however, is the most common metal to be found in the Earth's crust. The thing that made aluminium so dear was that it was very difficult to extract it from the rocks.

Metal ores

Almost all metals are found in the ground as ores, not as the shiny metal. People found how to get iron out of iron ore thousands of years ago. The same is true for copper, lead and zinc. All they had to do was heat the ore with carbon and the metal came out. This doesn't work with aluminium ore.

Iron is extracted from iron ore.

Using electricity

Just over a hundred years ago, a young man called Charles Hall was studying chemistry. His professor told the class about aluminium. He told them that the person who invented a cheap way of getting aluminium from its ore would make a fortune.

Hall worked out that metals could be extracted by melting the ore and passing electricity through it. He built a furnace in his backyard, melted some aluminium ore and then passed electricity through it. It worked! Shiny metallic aluminium was formed. This method of extracting aluminium is still used today. It is called the Hall Process.

Electricity is used to extract aluminium from its ore in factories like this.

Hall became a rich man because of his invention. The original aluminium that he extracted can still be seen at the headquarters of the Aluminium Company of America. Several other metals, including copper, are extracted by melting their ores and passing electricity through them.

Molten aluminium collects in the bottom of the cell when electricity is passed through the ore.

molten aluminium ore

molten aluminium

plug

Natural electricity

Electricity doesn't just come from batteries or generators. All living things create electricity. As you read this book, light from the page is entering your eye. The light hits the retina at the back of your eye and messages travel along the nerves to your brain.

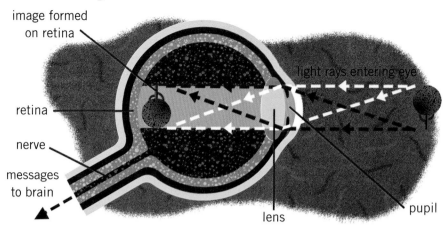

image formed on retina

light rays entering eye

retina

nerve

messages to brain

lens

pupil

Light goes into the eye and falls on the nerve cells at the back. This makes them send electrical messages to the brain.

Electrical messages

These messages are electrical. The same sort of thing happens when you touch, taste, smell or hear something. Electrical messages travel to your brain to tell you what is happening.

Imagine you have seen a sweet. The electric current passes along your nerves to your brain. A lot of electrical activity then goes on in your brain. It is called thinking. You decide to pick up the sweet. Electric currents go down another set of nerves to the muscles in your arm, hand and fingers to make them move in the right direction.

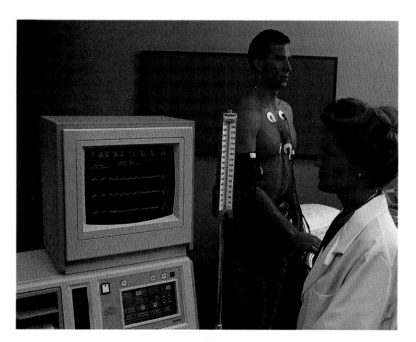

Detecting the messages

Electric currents are moving along the nerves in your body all the time. They tell you what is going on outside your body and they make your muscles respond. These electric currents are not very big, but they can be detected. If electrodes are fastened to a person's skin, the currents can be picked up and then made to move a pen on a rolling sheet of paper. Hospitals use machines to do this. They call it ECG.

If the electrodes are placed on the head, it is possible to get an idea of activity in the brain.

Electrical activity in the body can be picked up by this ECG machine.

Picking up the beat

Some people's hearts have an irregular beat.
A pacemaker can be fitted to give a steady electrical pulse of electricity to the heart muscles. This makes sure that the heart beats regularly and doesn't suddenly speed up or slow down.

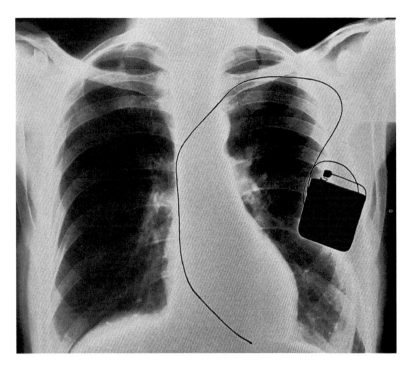

This X-ray shows that a pacemaker has been fitted to keep the heart beating regularly.

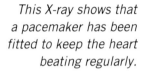

Animal generators

All animals depend on electric currents in their nerves. The currents are very small in most animals, but there are fish that can produce quite large amounts of electricity. One of these is the electric eel that lives in rivers in South America. It sends out electrical pulses through the water to find its prey.

To kill its prey, the eel has thousands of special cells in its tail. These can produce up to six hundred volts – more than twice the voltage of the mains supply in your home. Shocking, isn't it?

Electric eels can give electric shocks to other animals. The shocks are big enough to kill a human being.

Published by BBC Educational Publishing, BBC White City,
201 Wood Lane, London W12 7TS

First published 1997
© Mike Clemmet/BBC Worldwide (Educational Publishing) 1997
The moral right of the author has been asserted.

Paperback: 0 563 37308 3
Hardback: 0 563 37309 1

Colour reproduction by Goodfellow & Egan Ltd, England
Cover origination by Tinsley Robor, England
Printed and bound by Cambus Litho, Scotland

Acknowledgements

Illustrations: © Terry Kennett 1997 (pages 3, 9, 15, 18, 26, 27, 30
(top backgrounds) and 46); © Diane Lumley 1997 (pages 6, 8, 10
(bottom right), 16, 32, 33 and 40); © Salvatore Tomaselli 1997 (pages
10 (top and bottom left), 11–14, 21, 23, 24, 30 (bottom), 31, 34, 35,
37–9, 43 and 45)

Photos: © Catherine Ashmore **p. 24**; BBC Educational Publishing/John
Jefford **pp. 14, 20 (top)**; BBC Educational Publishing/Simon Pugh
**pp. 2, 6, 13, 17 (bottom), 19 (bottom), 20 (middle & bottom), 25, 27, 28,
29 (top), 36, 38 (top), 42, 43, 44 (top)**; Collections/Alain le Garsmeur
p. 17 (top); Collections/George Wright **p. 16**; Collections/John Miller
p. 22; Leslie Garland Picture Library/A. Lambert **pp. 4 (inset), 7 (main),
44 (bottom)**; Leslie Garland Picture Library/L. Garland **pp. 7 (inset), 19
(top)**; Mary Evans Picture Library **p. 4 (main)**; National Power Picture
Unit **p. 35**; NHPA/Norbert Wu **p. 47 (bottom)**; Pictor International **p. 5
(middle)**; Science Photo Library/Adam Hart-Davis **p. 5 (top)**; Science
Photo Library/Keith Kent **p. 5 (bottom)**; Science Photo Library/NASA
p. 29 (bottom); SuperStock **p. 38 (bottom)**; Tony Stone Images/A & L
Sinibaldi **p. 41 (bottom)**; Tony Stone Images/Chris McCooey **p. 41 (top)**;
Tony Stone Images/Greg Pease **p. 45**; Tony Stone Images/RNHRD NHS
Trust **p. 47 (top)**; Zefa Picture Library (UK) **pp. 31, 46**

Front cover: Telegraph Colour Library **(main)**; BBC Educational
Publishing/Simon Pugh **(inset)**